Father of the Bride

The Wedding Mentor, Volume 2

Wedding Mentor

Published by Story Ninjas, 2022.

While every precaution has been taken in the preparation of this book, the publisher assumes no responsibility for errors or omissions, or for damages resulting from the use of the information contained herein.

FATHER OF THE BRIDE

First edition. June 12, 2022.

ISBN: 979-8201838966

Written by Wedding Mentor.

Table of Contents

Father of the Bride
How To Give A Killer Wedding Speech
Tools, Tips, And Tricks To Create A Memorable Moment
By The Wedding Mentor

Copyright

THE PROBLEM WITH BEING THE FATHER OF THE BRIDE

IF YOU'RE READING THIS book, there's a good chance you've been chosen to be the father of the bride for a wedding.

Congratulations!

You just got suckered into doing a ton of work...

Seriously though, it goes without saying that the father of the bride has one of the most difficult jobs in the entire wedding party. Aside from the officiant, and perhaps the best man, the Father of the Bride's duties are by far the most numerous and diverse. From holding rings and coordinating with catering personnel, to handling last-minute "fires", and mingling with guests, the title of Father of the Bride carries with it a long list of responsibilities.

Chief among them is your Father of the Bride speech.

For anyone who's attended weddings before, you've probably seen the good, the bad, and the ugly. Some speakers give great speeches that energize the crowd and leave a memory that will last a lifetime. While others fumble through notes and put the audience to sleep. Worst of all is when a speaker fails so epically, that they leave people feeling awkward or uncomfortable. Intentional or not, this can have a long-lasting effect that taints the entire day for years to come. Whether it's broken microphones, drunken stumbling, or lack of preparation, there are a million things that can go wrong during the Father of the Bride speech.

This book aims to help you navigate the common pitfalls most fathers of the bride make, and help you give a killer Father of the Bride speech. In this book, I'll teach you how to prepare, brainstorm, outline, rehearse, and execute your speech. We'll discuss all of the duties of the father of the bride so you're completely prepared for the day of the wedding. This will include coordinating with the groom and bride, dress and appearance, interacting with friends and family, recording the speech, alcohol consumption and so much more. Additionally, you'll learn the most common issues that happen during the Father of the Bride speech and how to overcome them. Moreover, I provide an example speech at the end of the book, that can be tweaked for your particular needs.

Ultimately, this book will provide fathers of the bride with the tools, tips, tricks—and most importantly the confidence—they'll need to give a killer speech. By the end of the event, you'll walk out feeling like a hero and knowing you gave it 110%.

Nanny's Dried and Fried Fruit Pies (Whatever fruit or fruits you like)

Dough:

1 teaspoon salt

1 cup Crisco or other good vegetable shortening

1 beaten egg

$\frac{1}{4}$ cup cold water

1 teaspoon white vinegar

Mix together flour and salt. Mix in the shortening until the mixture looks crumbly. Stir beaten egg together with water then add to dough base. Add in the vinegar, mixing just enough until everything is combined. Plastic wrap the dough and refrigerate it for an hour or so.

Filling:

Each cup of dried fruit requires $\frac{1}{2}$ cup of water and two tablespoons of sugar. You may need to increase or decrease this based on the fruit you use.

3 cups dried fruit

1 $\frac{1}{2}$ cups water

6 tablespoons sugar

$\frac{1}{4}$ teaspoon cinnamon

$\frac{1}{4}$ teaspoon all-spice

On low heat, cook the dried fruit until soft, about 30 minutes or so (time will vary according to the fruit used). With a potato masher or big fork, mash the fruit up and mix in sugar, cinnamon and all-spice. See dough and frying section for the next steps.

Chocolate Fried Pies

Ingredients

Old-Fashioned Hot Kitchen Blueberry Fried Pies

Ingredients:

Dough:

2 cups of flour

$\frac{1}{2}$ teaspoon salt

$\frac{1}{2}$ cup of chilled lard

$\frac{1}{4}$ cup of cold water

Filling:

2 cups of fresh or frozen blueberries

$\frac{1}{2}$ cup of sugar

3 tablespoons of flour

1 teaspoon of lemon juice

$\frac{1}{2}$ teaspoon of cinnamon

$\frac{1}{2}$ cup of water

Directions:

Prepare the dough. Once your dough is chilling, combine all ingredients into a saucepan. Bring it to boil over medium heat for a few minutes.

Spoon filling into the center of each pre-cut piece of dough. Fold over the crust, sealing the filling inside, then pinch the edges closed with a fork or your fingers. See the dough and frying section at the front of the book for the next steps.

Quickie Crisp Pies

This is the fast-and-dirty version of fried pies. It's incredibly easy and very basic. It involves a package of refrigerator pie crusts and a big can of any kind of pie filling – any kind. Just remember to leave room around the pie filling for a good seal.

See the dough and frying section at the front of the book for the next steps.

Fried Dried Apple Biscuit Hand Pies

Ingredients:

8 ounces dried apples

1 cup water

$^1/_3$ cup sugar

1 tablespoon butter

1 can flake-like refrigerated biscuits

vegetable oil, for frying

Directions:

Combine apples and water in saucepan; bring to a boil. Cover, reduce heat, and simmer for 30 or until soft and mashable. Turn off heat, allow to cool and then use a large fork or potato masher to further pulp the cooked apples. Fold in the sugar and butter and mix.

Place each biscuit on a lightly floured surface. Smash it out into the right size (put two or more together if you like larger pies). Place a tablespoon of apple mixture on half of each biscuit, fold over to cover the apple filling, then press the biscuit edges together with a fork or your fingers (be careful, it's hot).
See the dough and frying section at the front of the book for the next steps.
Makes about a dozen pies.

$^1/_4$ cup all purpose flour

$^1/_2$ cup granulated sugar

$^1/_4$ cup powdered cocoa

$^1/_4$ teaspoon salt

$^1/_2$ cup milk

1 teaspoon vanilla

2 tablespoons butter

2 cups Bisquick or similar baking mix

$^1/_3$ cup milk

Directions:

Mix together flour, sugar, salt and powdered cocoa in saucepan. Add milk and butter. At moderate flame, cook until the contents boil for a couple of minutes. Add vanilla. Let cool.

Mix baking mix with milk. Roll out a thin layer of pastry dough over a flat, floured surface. Cut into sections, place a tablespoon of chocolate filling on each piece of dough, then fold it over to enclose the filling. Pinch or press the edges to seal them.

Heat oil in skillet and then carefully lower pies into the heated oil with a spatula. They're done when they're golden brown. Serve as suggested in section one.

Fried Cream Pies

Ingredients:

Filling:

1 cup milk

$^1/_4$ cup sugar

Pinch of salt

1 teaspoon butter

4 teaspoon cold water

2 beaten egg yolks

1 teaspoon vanilla

4 teaspoon cornstarch

Mix together the milk, sugar, salt and butter. Turn up heat to medium and cook until the mixture boils. In a separate bowl, combine cornstarch and water and then add to the other pan.   Cook over a low flame until the contents thicken. Add egg yolks and vanilla, then cook another 3-4 minutes. Allow to cool.

Dough:

2 tablespoon butter

1 cup sifted flour

1 egg yolk

3 tablespoon hot milk

Pinch of salt

Combine butter, flour, egg yolk, milk and salt to form the dough. Knead until well blended. Roll into $^1/_6$ to $^1/_8$ inch thick and cut into sections. Place 1 tablespoon of filling in the middle of each, folding it over and sealing them by pinching or crimping along the edges.

See <u>the dough and frying section</u> at the front of the book for the next steps.

Fried Cherry Nut Pies (no, Paula Deen didn't invent them)

Ingredients:

Vegetable oil

1 cup white sugar

$^2/_3$ cup light corn syrup

$^1/_3$ cup of clarified butter

2 eggs

1 1/2 cups nuts of your choice (walnuts work well)

1 teaspoon vanilla extract

Pinch of salt

$^1/_2$ cup finely chopped dried cherries

Small amount of flour

2 refrigerated pie crusts

Directions:

In a medium-sized saucepan, mix together sugar, corn syrup, melted butter and 2 eggs. Add nuts, vanilla and salt. Over a medium flame, bring the contents to a gentle boil. Lower the flame and simmer for ten minutes. Finally, add in the cherries and allow to cool for a half hour.

Unroll pie crusts onto flat and floured surface, cut into sections, place a portion of cherry nut mixture on dough, then fold over to seal in the filling. Pinch or crimp the edges. See the dough and frying section at the front of the book for the next steps.

Arkansas Blue Ribbon Apple Jack Fried Apple Pies

Ingredients

Dough:

3 cups all-purpose flour

2 teaspoons salt

2 teaspoons sugar

1 cup ice-cold unsalted butter

$\frac{1}{4}$ cup ice-cold lard, quartered

10 tablespoons ice water

Directions

In a large mixing bowl, stir together flour, salt and sugar. Put half of the butter and lard into the flour until they are lightly coated. Squish it all together until everything is blended. Add the rest of the butter and lard into the mixture.

Add in two tablespoons of the water to compel the dough to stick together.
Wrap the ball of dough in plastic wrap and put it in the fridge to get very cold while making filling.

Filling:

4 tablespoons unsalted butter

4 tablespoons light brown sugar

1 cup granulated sugar

$\frac{1}{4}$ cup apple brandy

6 peeled, cored and chopped up Granny Smith apples

1 tablespoon lemon juice

3 tablespoons cinnamon

4 cups Canola oil

In a large saucepan, melt the butter. Add the brown sugar and continue to heat, stirring until the mixture thickens. Pour in the apple brandy and cook for a minute or so longer.

Fold in the apples and cook for several minutes. Mix in the lemon juice, cinnamon and ginger with the apples until they are soft, cooked through and caramelized.

Pour onto baking sheet and let cool while preparing dough cut-outs for pies.
Roll out the dough on a flat, floured surface to cut out wedge-shaped dough
pieces for pies – or simply tear up the dough, make smallish balls and flatten
each out with your hand. Fold over the dough piece to enclose the apple
filling.   Crimp or pinch the edges of the dough to close.

See the dough and frying section at the front of the book for the next steps.

Coconut Cream Fried Pies

Ingredients:

1 cup whole milk

1 cup coconut milk

$\frac{1}{2}$ cup cream of coconut

$\frac{1}{4}$ cup cornstarch

Pinch of salt

2 eggs

1 $\frac{1}{2}$ cups toasted shredded coconut

2 tablespoons unsalted butter

$\frac{1}{2}$ teaspoon vanilla extract

1 recipe dough of your choosing

Melted chocolate

Toasted shredded coconut

Heat cow's milk and coconut milk in a pan over medium until they begin to bubble. Set aside to cool a little. In a bowl, mix together cream of coconut, cornstarch and salt. Add eggs, mixing until blended, gradually adding in half of the hot milk mixture (leave the rest in the pan). Pour the eggs-and-milk combined mixture into the rest of the milk in the pan. Cook over medium flame until it is thick. Take the pan off the burners and stir in one cup of the shredded coconut along with the vanilla and butter. Pour into a bowl and chill until cold. See the dough and frying section at the front of the book for the next steps. Garnish with melted chocolate and toasted coconut.

Deep Fried Cherry Mini-Pies

(makes about a dozen small or half-dozen larger pies)

2 $\frac{1}{2}$ cups all-purpose flour

Pinch of salt

1 cup ice-cold unsalted butter, quartered

4 tablespoons ice water

In a bowl, combine the flour and salt. Add in butter until dough appears crumbly Add water until dough adheres together. Knead dough into the shape of a ball. Cut into two parts. Cover with plastic wrap and refrigerate for several hours.

Filling:

4 cups fresh cherries, pitted

1 $\frac{1}{2}$ cups ice water

$\frac{1}{4}$ cup cornstarch

$\frac{3}{4}$ cup granulated sugar

Pinch of salt

2 tablespoons lemon juice

$\frac{1}{4}$ teaspoon vanilla extract

$\frac{1}{4}$ teaspoon cinnamon

Add together cherries, water, sugar, salt, lemon juice and cornstarch in a saucepan. Heat over medium flame until ingredients come to a boil. Reduce flame to low and cook while stirring about 15 minutes. Add in vanilla and cinnamon. Set aside to cool thoroughly.

Take dough from refrigerator and place it on a flat and floured surface. Roll out with rolling pin, cut into dough wedges, spoon a tablespoon of filling onto the dough wedges, folding over the filling and sealing it along the edges. See the dough and frying section at the front of the book for the next steps.

Nutella Fried Pies

1 tin of biscuit dough (could probably also be done with regular pie dough)

1 jar of Nutella

Powdered sugar/Sugar and cinnamon for garnish

Flatten down each biscuit, spread out a tablespoon of Nutella onto the biscuits, fold over the biscuit with the Nutella inside then seal around edges by pinching with your fingers or using a form.

Heat a skillet with sufficient oil with medium flame then carefully lower the little pies into the hot oil. Flip once when golden brown. These brown slowly, so take care to keep an eye on them.

Drain on paper towels or napkins and garnish with powdered sugar or cinnamon and sugar.

Fried Apricot Pie

Ingredients:

7 ounces of dried apricots

$\frac{2}{3}$ cup granulated sugar

$\frac{1}{2}$ cup water

1 tablespoon butter

1 can of regular biscuits (cheap type is fine)

Confectioners sugar

Cooking oil

Heat fruit, granulated sugar and $\frac{1}{2}$ cup water in a saucepan.

In a saucepan, combine fruit, sugar and 1/2 cup water. Cook over medium flame until fruit is soft and mixture is boiled down. Mash with large fork or potato masher. Add butter. Shut off heat and set aside to cool.

Place biscuits out on a floured surface and gently punch down with fist. Place 1 tablespoon (or more, if desired) of filling on each biscuit. Fold the biscuit over to enclose the filling and pinch around the edges to seal.

Fry slowly over medium flame until golden brown, turning once.

Garnish and serve as desired.

Buttery Fried Chocolate Pies

3 tablespoons cocoa

$\frac{1}{2}$ cup granulated sugar

$\frac{1}{2}$ stick of butter, melted

Any pie dough

Blend together cocoa, sugar and butter. Allow to cool. Cut out the pie wedges from your pie. Spoon 1 tablespoon onto each dough wedge. Fold over, sealing the chocolate filling inside. Crimp edges with fork or pinch with fingers. See the dough and frying section at the front of the book for the next steps.

Traditional Glazed Amish Fry Pies

Makes about 3 dozen pies

Ingredients:

9 cups of cake flour

2 tablespoons granulated sugar

1 tablespoon salt

3 cups vegetable shortening

2 cups water

Pie filling of your choice

Shortening or oil for frying

Glazuur (Glaze):

8 pounds confectioners sugar

$\frac{1}{2}$ cup cornstarch

$\frac{1}{3}$ cup powdered milk

1 teaspoon vanilla extract

2 $\frac{1}{2}$ cup warm water

In large bowl, mix together flour, sugar and salt. Mix in 3 cups of vegetable shortening until the mixture is crumbly. Gradually add water to moisten the flour mixture. When dough is balled up in one piece, pull it apart to make 10 dough wedges of more. Spoon pie filling into each wedge, folding the dough over the filling to seal it inside. Pinch or crimp edges to seal. See the dough and frying section at the front of the book for the next steps.

While the pie are cooling, mix all the glaze ingredients in a bowl. While the pies are still warmish, dip each one into the glaze. Let dry and cool on a wire rack or similar surface.

Fried Blackberry Pies

Filling:

Six quarts of blackberries

7 cups granulated sugar (may need 8 if berries are out of season or tart)

1 $^{3}/_{4}$ cups Clearjel starch (for thickening)

1 teaspoon cinnamon

9 $^{1}/_{3}$ cups water

Wash berries and pour into mixing bowl then set aside. Combine Clearjel, sugar and cinnamon in a saucepan. Add in water and stir until smooth. Heat on low flame, stirring constantly to preserve the thickening process. When bubbles start showing, pull off of heat and pour in berries.

See the dough and frying section at the front of the book for the next steps.

Aunt Nadine's Fried Nectarine-Blueberry Pies
(makes 40 pies)

Ingredients:

5 ripe nectarines

6 cups fresh blueberries

3 $\frac{1}{2}$ cups sugar

1 $\frac{1}{3}$ cups quick-cooking tapioca

1 teaspoon grated ginger

$\frac{1}{2}$ teaspoon cinnamon

$\frac{1}{6}$ teaspoon ground nutmeg

2 $\frac{1}{4}$ cups water

$\frac{3}{4}$ cup lemon juice

Directions:

Wash nectarines, halve, remove pits and cut into $\frac{1}{2}$ inch slices. Wash and drain blueberries.

In a big saucepan, heat six cups of water to a boil. Add in half of the nectarines and continue to boil for a minute. Spoon out nectarines into a large mixing bowl and cover it.

Pour out the water from the saucepan and mix together in it sugar, tapioca, ginger, cinnamon and nutmeg. Mix in 2 $\frac{1}{4}$ cups water. Allow to stand for a few minutes for tapioca to blend. Over high flame, stir constantly until mixture thickens and starts to bowl. Add lemon juice and boil for one minute. Add all the fruit, stirring to make certain it's all combined. Stir for a few minutes until the mixture is heated.

See the dough and frying section at the front of the book for the next steps.

Fried Pumpkin Hand Pies
Ingredients:

1 recipe pie dough

Pumpkin Vanilla Filling:

1 15 ounce can pumpkin puree

1 cup brown sugar

1 tablespoon vanilla bean paste

1 teaspoon cinnamon

½ nutmeg

½ ginger

½ teaspoon salt

1 cup cream

2 eggs

1 quart of vegetable oil for frying

Directions:

Preheat oven to 375 °

Combine all filling ingredients in a mixing bowl, making certain the mixture is well-blended, then pour it into a small, square baking pan. Bake pumpkin filling for about 45 minutes. Remove from stove and set aside to cool.

See the dough and frying section at the front of the book for the next steps. Great garnished with cinnamon sugar.

Pumpkin Pie Wontons

Serves 10-15

Ingredients:

1 15 ounce can pumpkin pie filling (NOT canned pumpkin – this is the pre-blended, ready-to pour into pie shell stuff)

2 eggs

$\frac{1}{2}$ cup sugar

2 teaspoons cinnamon

32 wonton wrappers

1 tablespoon water

Vegetable or canola oil, for frying

Directions:

Pour pumpkin pie filling into a mixing bowl. Add in 1 egg and stir until well combined.

Place the wonton wrappers on a flat work surface. Spoon a tablespoon of pie filling onto each wrapper. In a second bowl, beat together the other egg and water for a traditional egg wash. As with other wontons, brush the other edge of the wrapper with the egg wash. Fold the wrapper in half to enclose the filling. Pinch or crimp the edges to seal.

Pour a couple of inches of vegetable oil into a saucepan. Over a medium flame, heat the oil. Add wontons a few at a time into the hot oil. Fry until they are golden brown on both sides. Carefully remove the wontons from the oil and line across some paper napkins.

In another bowl, pour in the sugar and cinnamon. (You can also pour them into a shake-n-bake bag).

Coat them with cinnamon-sugar and serve. Be careful to let them cool before serving – the only thing hotter than hot fruit filling is hot pumpkin!)

Fried Pecan Pie

Serves 12

Ingredients:

$\frac{1}{3}$ cup softened butter

$\frac{1}{2}$ cup granulated sugar

$\frac{1}{4}$ cup light corn syrup

1 tablespoon self-rising flour

$\frac{1}{4}$ teaspoon salt

1 teaspoon vanilla extract

1 cup chopped pecans

1 package refrigerated pie dough

Directions:

Combine butter and sugar, creaming them together, then add in corn syrup, flour, salt and vanilla extract. Add in pecans. Stir until everything is combined.

See the dough and frying section at the front of the book for the next steps.

Fried Georgia Sweet Potato Pies

Serves 25

Dough:

4 ½ cups self-rising flour

3 tablespoons sugar

½ cup shortening

2 eggs

1 cup whole milk

Filling:

3 cups mashed sweet potatoes

2 cups granulated sugar

3 beaten eggs

1 5 oz can evaporated milk

¼ cup melted butter

3 tablespoons all-purpose flour

1 teaspoon vanilla extract

Oil for deep-fat frying

Powdered sugar for garnish, if desired.

Directions

Mix together flour and sugar in a bowl then add in shortening, mixing until the mixture looks crumbly. Add in eggs and milk, mixing until a dough ball forms. Wrap in plastic wrap and refrigerate for four to five hours.

In another bowl, blend together the seven filling ingredients.

Remove the dough from refrigerator and divide up into multiple little portions of the size you desire. On a floured surface, pound down each mini-ball to a flat wedge. Spoon 1 tablespoon of filling on each, then fold over the dough to enclose the filling, crimping or pinch the edges to seal. With a toothpick or fork, pierce each pie gently three times to release built-up steam so they won't crack.

Heat up the oil in a large pan. Gradually fry the pies until golden brown on each side. Drain on paper napkins or paper towels. Roll in powdered sugar if desired.

Insanely Delicious Old Southern Fried Chocolate Pies

Simple chocolate pie filling:

$^1/_2$ cup Hershey's cocoa powder

1 $^1/_8$ cup granulated sugar

$^1/_3$ cup cornstarch

1 teaspoon salt

3 cups of whole milk

3 tablespoons of butter

1 $^1/_2$ teaspoon vanilla extract

Combine in a saucepan the cocoa, granulated sugar, cornstarch and sale then mix together. Gradually stir in milk to blend with the cocoa and other ingredients in saucepan. Over medium flame, stir mixture until it boils. Boil for 60 seconds and then turn off the heat. Remove from stove. Add into the mixture the butter and vanilla. Stir well. Chill in refrigerator a few hours until firm.

Dough:

2 cups flour

1 teaspoon salt

$^1/_2$ cup Crisco

$^1/_2$ cup whole milk

Blend the vegetable shortening into the flour and salt, scrunching it with your fingers, the old-fashioned way (okay, you can use a fork if you want). Add in and stir. Divide the dough into multiple balls, flatten on a hard surface with a fist. See the dough and frying section at the front of the book for the next steps. (No need to chill the dough)

Good Bourbon Fried Apple Pies

Makes about 12 pies

Filling:

1 tablespoon unsalted butter

$^2/_3$ cup light brown sugar

$^1/_2$ teaspoon ground cinnamon

$^1/_2$ teaspoon all-spice

1 teaspoon vanilla extract

$^1/_2$ cup bourbon

6 apples peeled and chopped

1 large egg

1 recipe sugar pastry, to follow

Canola oil for frying

Sweet Pastry

1 cup all-purpose flour

1 cup cake flour

$^1/_2$ cup powdered sugar

Pinch of salt

1 stick unsalted butter softened at room temperature

3 large eggs

Add the flour (both kinds), sugar and salt in a food processor to combine, or use a hand mixer. Fold in butter and blend (in processor or with mixer) until the flour mix has a crumbly appearance.

In a second bowl, beat the eggs. Add in the eggs over the flour and pulse or mix until the mixture is clumpy. Ball up the dough, wrap it in plastic wrap and refrigerate well for four hours.

In a heavy pan over a medium flame, mix together butter, cinnamon, all-spice, brown sugar and vanilla. Boil for several minutes until caramelized (is brown and thicker like caramel).

Take the pan off the stove to add in the bourbon, then place it back over medium flame, cooking and stirring for a few minutes. You may need to stir for several minutes to blend everything sufficiently.

Fold in apples, making certain the apples are coated with the pan contents. Cook for five more minutes, take off the stove and allow to cool.

Beat together the egg and $\frac{1}{2}$ cup of cold water then set it aside. Roll out the sweet dough on a flat and floured surface. Cut the dough into wedges for pies. Spoon some of the apple mixture onto the sweet pastry wedges. Fold over the wedge, enclosing the filling, and seal the edges with your fingers or crimping with a fork.

Fried a few at a time in hot oil, turning once until both sides are golden brown. Drain on paper towels.

You can use the egg wash to give the fried pies extra luster after they've cooled.

Cinnamon and sugar or powdered sugar for garnish.

Aunt Retha's Nothing Fancy Fried Blueberry Pie

Filling:

2 cups fresh or frozen blueberries

$\frac{1}{2}$ cup granulated sugar

3 tablespoons all-purpose flour

1 teaspoon lemon juice

$\frac{1}{2}$ teaspoon cinnamon

$\frac{1}{2}$ cup water

Directions:

In a saucepan, combine all the filling ingredients and bring them to a boil. Simmer for three minutes.

See the dough and frying section at the front of the book for the next steps.

Fried Strawberry Pie

2 cups fresh or thawed strawberries

$^3/_4$ cup granulated sugar

$^1/_4$ cup cornstarch

1 package Pillsbury refrigerated pie crusts

Canola oil

Confectioners sugar

Preparation

Mash up strawberries with a potato masher or large form. Fold the mashed strawberries into a saucepan, adding the sugar and cornstarch. Bring to a boil. Cook, stirring until thickened. Set aside to cool.

See the dough and frying section at the front of the book for the next steps.

Fried Fig Pies (can also be fried prune pies)

Filling:

1 cup dried figs

2 cups water

1 cup sugar

$\frac{1}{4}$ cup butter

1 tablespoon lemon juice

$\frac{1}{2}$ teaspoon cinnamon

Simmer together figs (or prunes) and water, bringing the mixture to a boil. Reduce flame and simmer until fruit is soft. Mash together butter, lemon juice and cinnamon. Set aside to cool.

See the dough and frying section at the front of the book for the next steps.